CW01431839

Original title:

Luminous Quips Around the Unicorn Mesh

Copyright © 2025 Swan Charm

Author: Liina Liblikas

ISBN HARDBACK: 978-1-80562-734-0

ISBN PAPERBACK: 978-1-80564-255-8

Celestial Laughter in Starlit Gardens

In gardens where the starlight sings,
Moonbeams dance on shadowed wings,
Petals blush in twilight's gaze,
While laughter echoes through the haze.

Whispers weave through fragrant blooms,
As night unfolds its mystic plumes,
The silvery dewdrops softly glow,
Beneath the sky's enchanting show.

Each twinkle holds a tale to share,
Of secrets floating in the air,
Where time and dreams entwine and bind,
In gardens where the stars unwind.

A cosmic breeze caresses grace,
As hearts entwine in this bright space,
With every sigh, the cosmos speaks,
In laughter's song, the magic peaks.

Twinkling Tales of Fantastical Beasts

In woods where shadows twist and twine,
A tapestry of tales benign,
With creatures bright and legends bold,
The stories of the night unfold.

Dragonflies with jeweled wings,
Flutter by as moonlight sings,
While unicorns in silence tread,
On paths where only dreams have led.

A phoenix glows with fiery grace,
Her vibrant plume, a rare embrace,
As whispers of the wildest dreams
Float softly on the silver streams.

Each rustle holds a heart's delight,
As magic stirs beneath the night,
In glimmering realms where wonder gleams,
And every beast is born from dreams.

Gossamer Light Beneath the Arcane Canopy

Beneath the boughs, where secrets dwell,
A gossamer light casts its spell,
The dialogue of leaf and breeze,
Tells stories lost among the trees.

Faint flickers dance like fireflies,
Illuminating ancient ties,
With every shimmer, a tale to weave,
In the heart of night, we dare believe.

The softest rustle, a tender plea,
From worlds unseen, inviting thee,
To wander wide through realms of lore,
And find the magic at the core.

In shadows deep, enchantments sing,
With every breath, the forests cling,
To light the path where spirits roam,
In whispers sweet, they call us home.

Sparkling Banter in Dreamy Groves

In groves where softest echoes play,
And dreams unfurl in bright array,
The banter sparkles like the dew,
A playful tune, both sweet and true.

With every step, the laughter twirls,
As magic in the twilight whirls,
A symphony of hearts in bloom,
Within this wondrous, fragrant room.

The nightingale with voice so clear,
Sings of hope, of love, of cheer,
While fireflies join in joyful flight,
To paint the canvas of the night.

In dreamy groves, we share the light,
With every shared and tender sight,
The world transforms, and we embrace,
In sparkling banter, time finds grace.

Radiant Footprints on Stardust Paths

Under the moon's soft glow,
Children of dreams tread lightly,
With radiant footprints aglow,
Across stardust paths, so brightly.

Whispers of magic in the air,
Enchantments twirl in the night,
Each twinkle a secret to share,
A dance of wonder, pure delight.

Through the veil of celestial gleam,
Courage beckons with each step,
Embracing the spark of a dream,
Where starlit wishes adeptly kept.

Floating on the breeze so sweet,
Laughter echoes, soft and clear,
Where heartbeats and joy entreat,
In stardust paths, there's no fear.

Hand in hand, they journey forth,
A constellation guiding their way,
With radiant footprints of worth,
In the magic of night, they sway.

Chasing Light Through Arcane Woods

In the shadows of ancient trees,
Where sunlight dares to play,
Chasing light on mischievous breeze,
The heart stirs with each bright ray.

Fungi glow in colors rare,
Secrets hide in every nook,
A symphony of magic in the air,
As if time's pages gently shook.

Rustling leaves whisper wayward lore,
Echoes of footsteps from long ago,
Dreams linger at the forest's core,
In the warm embrace of a golden glow.

Silhouettes dance, both wild and free,
Like spells cast under a veil,
Guided by the light's decree,
In this enchanted, timeless tale.

With laughter shared and dreams unfurled,
They forge ahead, hearts in flight,
In arcane woods, a magical world,
As they chase the elusive light.

Sparkling Snippets in an Echoing Grove

In the grove where echoes linger,
And sunlight kisses the leaves,
Sparkling snippets from slender fingers,
Weaving stories that the heart perceives.

A gentle breeze fans whispered lore,
As petals dance on the air,
Glimmers of magic, secrets galore,
In this enchanted realm, so rare.

Each step an adventure unfolds,
With fairies twinkling like stars,
In the sunlight, myths retold,
Captured in laughter, and moonlit bars.

Reflecting shards of dreams embraced,
The echoes hum through each glade,
A tapestry of joy interlaced,
In a world where memories won't fade.

As twilight beckons, day turns to night,
The grove sings its comforting song,
In sparkling snippets, love ignites,
Together, they know where they belong.

Fantastical Murmurs Under a Glistening Sky

Under the vast, glistening sky,
Fantastical murmurs fill the air,
As day bids farewell with a sigh,
Dreams abound, fragile and rare.

Fireflies twinkle like stars in flight,
Guiding lost souls to the bright,
Woven in shadows, glimmers ignite,
As hope takes wing, from dusk till light.

In a meadow kissed by twilight's brush,
Where the cosmos bends to hear them speak,
Every heartbeat quickens, a thrilling rush,
In the embrace of all who seek.

Voices echo, soft and sweet,
Telling tales of love and lore,
In this realm where spirits meet,
As hearts dance upon the shore.

With every sigh, every whispered prayer,
Beneath the glistening expanse high,
Fantastical murmurs linger, rare,
In the tapestry of star-filled sky.

Cosmic Giggles in the Land of Wonder

In a land where stars do dance,
Laughter twinkles in each glance.
The moonbeams giggle, soft and bright,
Casting spells in the velvet night.

Whispers of the cosmic breeze,
Swaying gently through the trees.
Each leaf a secret, every sound,
In this magic, joy is found.

Rivers of stardust flow so wide,
With wishes swirling, side by side.
A kaleidoscope of dreams ignite,
Painting colors in the night.

Giggles echo, a symphony,
Binding hearts in harmony.
In the wonder, we all belong,
As the universe hums its song.

Through the realms where silence sings,
Imagination takes to wings.
With every chuckle, spirits soar,
In the land of wonder, forevermore.

Radiant Threads of Heartfelt Nonsense

In a tapestry of playful hues,
Dancing dreams adorn the views.
Each thread a tale, each knot a cheer,
Woven tightly, love draws near.

Silly whispers fill the air,
As whimsy wanders everywhere.
With a pinch of joy and dash of grace,
Heartfelt nonsense finds its place.

Giggles twine 'round every seam,
In this quilt of a wondrous dream.
The patterns twist, they spin and leap,
In a world where magic sleeps.

Underneath a sky of glee,
A carnival for you and me.
Radiant threads take flight and twirl,
In this delightful, dream-filled whirl.

Lost in laughter, found in love,
Like stars that shine from up above.
Each absurdity, a heartfelt key,
Unlocking joy for you and me.

Celestial Mischief in the Garden of Dreams

In a garden where wishes bloom,
Magic dances, casting gloom.
Cosmic sprites with playful grins,
Sprinkle mischief, where fun begins.

Softly twinkling, stars awake,
Whispers of laughter on the lake.
Petals giggle under the moon,
In this garden, all dreams are strewn.

Butterflies in a merry race,
Chase the fireflies in their space.
With each flutter, enchantments blend,
Celestial mischief knows no end.

Underneath the silver light,
Dreamers gather, hearts take flight.
In this realm of fanciful schemes,
We find our joy in woven dreams.

Every shadow hides a grin,
In this garden, we begin.
With each giggle and every cheer,
Celestial mischief whispers near.

Sparkling Fables from a Shimmering Dreamscape

In a dreamscape filled with sparkles bright,
Fables dance in the soft twilight.
Every story, a shimmering thread,
Unraveling tales that sparkle ahead.

Wizards chuckle, dragons play,
In this wonderland, night meets day.
Each whimsy cradled in moonlit beams,
Weaving destiny from our dreams.

Mystical creatures share their lore,
As starlight beckons us to explore.
With every fable spun anew,
Adventure calls for me and you.

In laughter's echo, hearts ignite,
Fables flourish in the night.
With a sprinkle of magic, all can see,
The shimmering dreams that set us free.

Whispers twirl on a golden breeze,
In this realm where wonders tease.
Sparkling tales forever gleam,
In the enchanting world of dreams.

Glistening Cryptics in Whimsical Peaks

In mountains high where echoes play,
The whispers of the breezes say,
A cryptic tale in twilight's glow,
Where secrets hide and wonders flow.

Glistening dreams on frosted stone,
Awake the truths that have been sown,
In shadows cast by twilight's seam,
A world unfolds, a silent dream.

With every step, the path reveals,
The magic that the heart conceals,
A dance of stars, a flicker bright,
In whimsical hues of silver light.

The peaks stand proud, with faces carved,
By ancient winds and tales starved,
In starlit grips, the stories find,
A symphony of the wise and kind.

So wander forth, let spirits rise,
In glistening cryptics, seek the skies,
For there in heights where dreams can spin,
The whimsy waits, just dive right in.

Dreamweaver's Revelry on Starry Nights

When darkness falls and stars ignite,
The dreamweaver spins tales in light,
With threads of silver, soft and bright,
He carves the wishes of the night.

The moon dons a cloak of shimmering grace,
Guiding lost souls in a sacred space,
Where laughter lives and shadows play,
In the revelry where dreams sway.

Beneath the gaze of starlit beams,
The heart embarks on wildest dreams,
As whispers of magic fill the air,
Unraveling hopes beyond compare.

With every twinkle, a secret shared,
In joyful circles, minds prepared,
To dance with fate in twilight's gleam,
In dreamweaver's hands, reality bends.

So when you find your heart takes flight,
Embrace the magic, hold on tight,
For in the depths of starry nights,
The dreamweaver calls with gentle lights.

Array of Lights in the Unicorn's Glade

In a glade where unicorns dance free,
An array of lights calls us to see,
With laughter bright and hooves of gold,
Their magic stories have yet to be told.

Amidst the blooms in colors rare,
The air is sweet, with dreams to share,
Each flicker whispers of wonder near,
As creatures gather, hearts sincere.

A shimmering path of glowing dew,
Leads to places known to few,
With every step, enchantments gleam,
Inviting all to chase a dream.

Together we'll weave the night so bright,
Where wishes soar and take their flight,
In the unicorn's glade, souls intertwine,
Embracing the magic, divine and fine.

So roam with joy, let spirits glide,
Through arrays of lights, we'll ever abide,
In the glade of dreams where hopes reside,
With unicorns as our faithful guide.

Brilliant Nonsense of the Enchanted Wood

In the heart of woods, where whispers are bold,
Lies brilliant nonsense, a tale to be told,
With trees that giggle and shadows that sway,
A place where the ordinary paves way.

The flowers gossip in colors so bright,
As fireflies dance in the velvet night,
Their laughter echoes through branches high,
Inviting the dreamers to step and fly.

Beneath the boughs where magic hums,
Creatures emerge with whimsical drums,
A symphony spun of curious cheer,
In enchanted woods, there's naught to fear.

With every rustle, a secret unfolds,
In the tales of the leaves, so sweetly retold,
The nonsense dances in laughter's embrace,
Enchanting the mind in a wondrous space.

So wander where the wild things play,
In the brilliant nonsense, drift and stay,
For in the heart of this enchanted wood,
Magic thrives where the child once stood.

Ethereal Whispers in Tinsel Dreams

In twilight's grace, the stars do sing,
A dance of light on silver wing.
Whispers soft, like secrets spun,
Tinsel dreams 'neath the watching sun.

Through shadows deep, the faeries glide,
With laughter sweet, they will not hide.
Cascading moons with gentle glow,
Guide the heart where wild winds blow.

A sparkling mist in the evening chill,
Ethereal realms with a heart to fill.
Lost in wonder, the night unfurls,
As dreams take flight in starlit swirls.

In every breath of the midnight air,
A promise made, a whispered prayer.
The world awakens, soft and bright,
In tinsel dreams, we own the night.

Glimmering Jest in Celestial Realms

In the dance of stars, a jest unfolds,
Glimmers of laughter, in night's hold.
With nebula spun in colors bold,
Weave tales of old, in stardust told.

Upon comet tails, we ride with glee,
Through celestial paths, forever free.
Madcap sprites in the heavens cavort,
With twinkling eyes, they twist and distort.

In every wink of the cosmos bright,
Echoes of joy burst forth, a light.
Adventure calls from beyond the sky,
Where dreams converge, and spirits fly.

The moonlight beckons with playful grace,
In glimmering jest, we find our place.
Through cosmic laughter, hearts will soar,
In the universe wide, we seek for more.

Radiant Reflections on Mythic Threads

Threads of gold, where stories weave,
Mythic tales that we believe.
Every whisper, a truth untold,
In radiant light, the past unfolds.

From ancient scrolls, the legends call,
Echoes of heroes who dared to fall.
Through valleys deep and mountains high,
Their spirits linger, never to die.

With every glance, the world awakes,
In the fabric of time, a memory breaks.
We gather strength from those who came,
Radiant reflections, igniting flame.

A quest through shadows, where dreams unite,
On mystic threads, we find our light.
With courage bold, we step ahead,
As hearts beat fierce for the stories spread.

Shimmering Echoes from Enchanted Fields

In fields where wildflowers sway and dance,
Shimmering echoes arise by chance.
A melody sung by the whispering breeze,
Caresses the soul, and the heart finds ease.

Beneath the canopy of dreams untold,
The magic of nature begins to unfold.
Each petal a note, each leaf a rhyme,
In enchanted fields, we conquer time.

Through twilight hues, a symphony flows,
A hint of laughter wherever it goes.
With every breath, the earth exhales,
In shimmering echoes, our spirit sails.

The promise of dawn in the morning light,
Guides us gently from the tender night.
With hearts aglow, and wishes sealed,
We dance in the magic of enchanted fields.

Celestial Whispers in the Enchanted Grove

In the grove where moonlight spills,
Secrets murmur through the hills.
Rustling leaves with tales to tell,
Echoes from a magic well.

Stars hang low, their glimmers bright,
Dance with shadows, soft and light.
Dreams take flight on gentle breeze,
Carried forth by ancient trees.

A silver stream reflects the sky,
Where whispers of the nightbirds fly.
Mystic creatures roam the night,
Guided by the starlit light.

From hidden nooks, old spirits sigh,
While fireflies weave tales up high.
Each rustle holds a story deep,
In the grove where secrets sleep.

Sparkling Secrets of the Mythical Horn

In a vale where legends sigh,
Lies the horn that echoes high.
Covered in the morning dew,
Whispers of the old so true.

Cascading notes of silver sound,
Enchantments in the air abound.
Creatures gather, eyes aflame,
For the horn holds magic's name.

With every note, a wish is cast,
Binding future, present, past.
Through twilight mist, its song takes flight,
Spreading warmth in endless night.

Adventurers seek its shining light,
To unveil mysteries, bold and bright.
In the echoes, destinies blend,
With the horn, the journey won't end.

Glimmers Beneath the Starlit Veil

Beneath the veil of twinkling stars,
Dreamers gather, near and far.
The night unfolds its glittering cloak,
Enveloping hearts with the words unspoke.

Luminous traces of wishful hopes,
In every shadow, a story copes.
As comet tails streak the skies,
Whispers of magic softly rise.

The moon, a guardian, watches near,
Casting solace, casting cheer.
With each heartbeat, the night expands,
Woven dreams in gentle hands.

Glimmers spark in every gaze,
Awakening paths through twilight haze.
In the dance of starlit streams,
Lies the world of boundless dreams.

Radiant Jests in the Realm of Dreams

In the realm where dreams take flight,
Radiant jesters spark delight.
With laughter swirling in the air,
Magic twinkles everywhere.

Mirthful faces, colors bright,
Turn the dark into pure light.
Each jest a secret, playfully spun,
Underneath the laughing sun.

Whimsical tales in their mirth unfold,
Stories of wishes, daring and bold.
In every giggle, a spell awakes,
Crafted from joy that never breaks.

From midnight's keep to dawn's first gleam,
They dance in shadows, bask in dream.
With each twirl, new wonders bloom,
In a realm where joys consume.

Whimsical Radiance of Magical Journeys

In forests deep where shadows play,
The whispered tales of night and day.
With lanterns bright and wands in hand,
We dance beneath the starry band.

Through twisting paths where fairies glide,
Each step we take, a world opens wide.
The laughter echoes, hearts aglow,
As magic blooms in every flow.

The creatures wink with mischief near,
In every corner, joy and cheer.
We twirl with gnomes, and sprites take flight,
In this enchanted, wondrous night.

A tapestry of dreams unwrought,
In every heartbeat, hope is sought.
Together, we weave a spell so bright,
A journey cloaked in pure delight.

Embrace the whimsy, chase the light,
In every corner, magic's sight.
With hearts wide open to the dream,
We'll soar on journeys, wild and free.

Illuminated Mirth Amongst Fantastical Creatures

In glades where laughter lifts the soul,
Fantastical beings play their role.
With giggles soft and twinkling eyes,
They share their secrets, wise and spry.

The unicorns graze on starlit dreams,
While playful sprites weave moonbeam seams.
Each moment bursts, a spark, a grin,
In a world where magic weaves within.

The echoes of a soft refrain,
In every dance, in joy, no pain.
A chorus blooms of mirth and song,
As friendships blossom, fierce and strong.

A dragon's roar, a gentle breeze,
In harmony, we find our ease.
The tapestry of jests and gleeful plays,
In every heart, the magic stays.

Together now, we roam the fields,
Where every truth the spirit yields.
The creatures of the night are near,
Illuminated, wrapped in cheer.

Dazzling Reflections in a Charmed Realm

In mirrors framed with silver lace,
We find reflections of our grace.
Each shimmer tells a tale anew,
In this charmed realm where dreams come true.

The rivers flow with stardust bright,
In every ripple, pure delight.
A world unveiled through crystal skies,
Where hope and magic never dies.

The landscapes twist like colors bold,
In every shadow, stories told.
We wander through the misty haze,
A maze of wonder, a show of rays.

Beneath the moons of silver glow,
A dance unwinds in soft, low flow.
With every twirl, the magic spins,
In laughter, joy, our journey begins.

In this enchanted realm, we stand,
With heart and spirit ever grand.
Dazzling reflections, pure and clear,
In our souls, we hold them dear.

Starlit Giggles Amidst Mystic Patterns

As stars adorn the velvet night,
We gather 'neath their twinkling light.
With giggles soft as whispers low,
In mystic patterns, secrets flow.

The constellations hum a tune,
As gentle breezes greet the moon.
We frolic while the shadows dance,
In every moment, pure romance.

A tapestry of dreams we weave,
In every heart, we dare believe.
The magic twirls like silken threads,
Where joy resides and sorrow treads.

The night unfolds with playful sprites,
In every corner, pure delights.
With starlit giggles, spirits soar,
In this enchanted world, we explore.

Amidst the patterns, secrets gleam,
The whispers spark a wondrous dream.
In every giggle, every sigh,
We find our wings and learn to fly.

Brilliance of Fantasy on Glistening Paths

In twilight's shimmer, dreams unfold,
With whispers soft, of tales untold.
Glistening paths where stardust plays,
In night's embrace, enchanting ways.

Wanderers roam in hope's sweet light,
Chasing shadows, taking flight.
Each footstep echoes, magic sings,
As fantasy weaves its golden strings.

Beneath the moon, secrets lie deep,
Unraveled wishes, never to sleep.
With every heartbeat, wonders sway,
In this realm where dreams hold sway.

Flowers bloom with laughter bright,
Casting colors in the night.
To live among the whispered dreams,
Is to awaken, or so it seems.

In the glimmer of magical skies,
Where hope ascends and fear just flies.
The brilliance dances, shadows part,
Forever igniting the restless heart.

Laughter That Dances on the Edge of Imagination

In realms where giggles spark delight,
A playful breeze takes fragile flight.
With every chuckle, colors blend,
A tapestry of joy, without end.

Whirling wisps of laughter rise,
Lighting up the moonlit skies.
In whispered banter, secrets gleam,
A vivid waltz, a waking dream.

Oh, taste the joy upon your tongue,
Where every story is sweetly sung.
On the edge of thoughts, they leap and play,
Creating magic, come what may.

With every tickle of the mind,
Imagination becomes unconfined.
For laughter is the bridge we seek,
To realms where wonder finds its peak.

As fleeting moments weave through time,
The rhythm of heartbeats, pure and prime.
Let laughter guide the way anew,
To worlds where dreams are born in hue.

Enchanted Threads of Glowing Whimsy

In twilight's glow, enchantments stir,
With threads of whimsy, hearts concur.
A tapestry where dreams take flight,
Woven in colors of pure delight.

Each stitch a story, rich and bold,
Of ancient secrets yet untold.
Through laughter's echoes, magic sways,
In this enchanted, timeless maze.

Beneath the stars, we dance and weave,
Finding treasures we believe.
In shadows deep, where dreams reside,
An artful journey we shall ride.

With every twirl, the past ignites,
A tapestry of starry nights.
From threads of whimsy, futures bloom,
Filling shadows with love's sweet perfume.

So thread by thread, we'll craft our fate,
With glowing wishes, never late.
In realms where whimsy paints the dawn,
The heart's true magic lingers on.

Celestial Musings in a Fanciful Realm

In the heart of dreams, where starlight glows,
Celestial musings gently flow.
Whispers of wonder fill the air,
As thoughts take wing in tapestry rare.

A fanciful realm, where shadows play,
Where time is lost, and worries sway.
With every heartbeat, galaxies spin,
In cosmos bright, where we begin.

Lost in the waltz of wonder's glow,
Where every tune is sweet to know.
Among the stars, our visions soar,
Unlocking dreams behind each door.

As moons converse in silvery night,
We'll dance on beams of brilliance bright.
With joyous hearts and open minds,
In this fanciful realm, true magic finds.

So come with me to where dreams dwell,
In celestial chambers, all is well.
In laughter's light, our souls take flight,
In fanciful realms of endless night.

Faerie Flickers of Joyous Fables

In whispers soft, the faeries dance,
Amidst the twinkling, bright expanse.
With laughter light and wings aglow,
They weave their tales in twilight's show.

Each flicker sparks a story spun,
Where magic glows and dreams are won.
In secret glades where shadows play,
A joyous fable finds its way.

With every flutter, night unfolds,
A tapestry of secrets told.
In starlit nights, their voices sing,
Of wondrous worlds and timeless spring.

Through silver mist, their laughter rings,
A heart that soars on faerie wings.
In every tale, a touch of light,
Where hopes arise and fears take flight.

So close your eyes, let dreams ignite,
In faerie fables, pure delight.
With every whisper, every glance,
Join in the magical dance.

Twilight Tales from the Enchanted Glade

In twilight's hush, the shadows blend,
Where ancient trees their stories send.
Beneath the boughs, where secrets lie,
Tales weave like stars across the sky.

The brook's soft murmur, gentle and clear,
Tells of laughter, love, and fear.
With every ripple, a tale begins,
Of lost adventures and timeless sins.

In the heart of glade, where moonlight gleams,
Dreams take shape in silvery beams.
Each rustling leaf, a whispered thought,
Of all the wonders that life has brought.

Creatures gather, old and wise,
To share their tales 'neath starlit skies.
In every glance, a magic spark,
Breathes life into the inky dark.

So listen close, and you may find,
The echoes of the faerie kind.
In twilight's grip, let stories flow,
From enchanted glades where hearts will glow.

Shining Dreams Across the Mystical Horizon

Beyond the hills, where dreams take flight,
A horizon glimmers, pure and bright.
With every dawn, new hopes arise,
Shining dreams in morning skies.

Across the fields, with colors bold,
Mystical wonders gently unfold.
In every step, a tale to share,
Of shimmering visions, beyond compare.

Through whispered winds, a promise sings,
Of endless joy and wondrous things.
Embrace the light, let worries cease,
In dreams we find our hearts' true peace.

As twilight dances in soft embrace,
The stars reveal a sacred place.
With every wish, the world expands,
Crafted by fate's skilled hands.

So chase the dawn, embrace the night,
For shining dreams glow, ever bright.
In the mystical embrace of time,
Each heartbeat flows, a lasting rhyme.

Silvery Smiles in the Land of Enchantment

In lands where silvery rivers flow,
And laughter echoes, sweet and low.
The flowers bloom in vibrant hues,
With every petal, joy infuse.

Beneath the trees, where shadows play,
The enchantment stirs in bright display.
Fairies giggle, their voices twine,
Revealing secrets, yours and mine.

The moonlight casts a glowing sheen,
On dreams awakened, never seen.
With each embrace, a magic smile,
Inviting hearts to linger awhile.

Across the glen, a spark ignites,
Creating warmth on chilly nights.
In silvery smiles, we find our way,
To endless joy where children play.

So wander forth, let spirits soar,
In the land of enchantment, evermore.
For every moment, every sigh,
Is woven into the azure sky.

Threads of Light Twirling in Magical Cadence

In the forest where whispers dwell,
The moon weaves tales with a shimmering spell.
Stars awash in twilight glow,
Binding secrets that none may know.

Moss carpets the paths of forgotten lore,
Where shadows dance and spirits soar.
Glimmers flicker through ancient trees,
A symphony played by a wandering breeze.

Each thread of light, a story spun,
Of realms where the wild and wonders run.
In the heart of the glade, magic sings,
As the night wraps around on silver wings.

Through the tapestry of dusk they weave,
Whispers of dreams that we dare believe.
In every tug, a spark ignites,
Threads of light threading through starry nights.

So dance with the echoes of time's embrace,
In the rhythm of a mystical place.
With every twirl, let your spirit take flight,
In the threads of light, pure and bright.

Gleeful Sparks from a Dreamer's Realm

In a world where wishes meet,
Gleeful sparks flit on nimble feet.
With colors vibrant, joy unleashed,
A tapestry of laughter, never ceased.

Chasing clouds with hearts so bold,
From golden dreams, new tales unfold.
In secret gardens, magic pools,
Where time abandons the rigid rules.

Fairies giggle beneath the stars,
Unleashing giggles, erasing scars.
With sparkling eyes, they glide and play,
Painting shadows into the day.

In the heart of the night, dreams entwine,
With gleeful sparks, the world divine.
Elders whisper of blessings rare,
As laughter dances through the air.

So gather 'round, let the magic bloom,
Where joy prevails, dispelling gloom.
In the dreamer's realm, let love ignite,
With gleeful sparks, a wondrous sight.

Dazzling Quirks Across a Twilight Canvas

Upon the canvas of twilight's breath,
Dazzling quirks bloom, defying death.
In hues of gold and hues of blue,
Each stroke sings of all that's true.

Whiskered shadows dance on the ground,
Where whimsical wonders can be found.
Chasing horizons where colors blend,
The quirk of life knows no end.

With starlit laughter echoing free,
Magic spills from the heart of the sea.
Eldritch forms leap and twirl,
In a fantastical, enchanted whirl.

Colors collide in a playful spree,
Draped in brilliance for all to see.
Nature's hand works its art in delight,
Across the canvas of endless night.

So come, embrace the shimmering dusk,
Where dreams are sparked, and visions discuss.
In the quirk of life, in soft advance,
Dazzling echoes call for a dance.

Enigmatic Flickers of Laughter in Avalon

In Avalon where whispers roam,
Enigmatic flickers find their home.
With laughter woven through the night,
Magic dances in sheer delight.

Beneath a sky of indigo dreams,
Where the brook sings in silver streams.
Elders gather with tales untold,
Crafting legends, both brave and bold.

Echoes of joy serenade the vale,
Championing hearts where wonders sail.
With every glance, a spark ignites,
Flickering laughter like fireflies' flights.

In shadows cast by the moonlit trees,
Resides a laughter that lightens the breeze.
Every chuckle, a luminous sign,
In the heart of Avalon, pure and divine.

So let your spirit soar through the night,
Awake to enchantments, to pure delight.
For in the flickers of joy we find,
The magic and mystery that life designed.

Silvery Echoes of Playful Mystique

In moonlit glades where soft winds play,
Whispers twirl as shadows sway.
A laughter lost in time's embrace,
Calls forth the dreams of a secret place.

Slivers of silver dance on the stream,
Glimmers of light, a fleeting dream.
Pixies frolic beneath the boughs,
In gentle whimsy, they take their vows.

Amidst the thickets where wildflowers bloom,
Mystique weaves around in fragrant plume.
The stars are strewn like memories dear,
As night unveils its magic near.

Each echo sings a tale untold,
Of joy and wonder, vibrant and bold.
In every rustle, a secret is shared,
In every flicker, a heart ensnared.

So wander here where spirits delight,
In silvery echoes that sail through the night.
For in this realm of playful charms,
Every heart finds solace in nature's arms.

Celestial Wonders of Whimsy and Delight

Beneath the heavens, stars take flight,
Sparking dreams in the velvet night.
Each twinkle tells a story bright,
Of wonders grand, of pure delight.

Clouds like castles drift on high,
Guarding secrets as time passes by.
In their shadow, giggles abound,
Hidden treasures waiting to be found.

Lunar beams weave soft and kind,
Casting hopes to hearts entwined.
With every flash, a wish is spun,
In this dance of light, we are all one.

Colors swirl in a vibrant waltz,
Nature's palette has no faults.
With every brush, harmony grows,
In every shade, true beauty flows.

So take a moment, breathe in this view,
Let the wonders awaken in you.
For above us lies a mystical tale,
Of celestial realms where dreams set sail.

Lighthearted Fables Beneath Glittering Skies

In fields adorned with daisies white,
Fables dance in the soft twilight.
Stories weave through each gentle breeze,
Whispered secrets among the trees.

A cozy nook where critters dwell,
Each has a tale they long to tell.
With every laugh, the shadows blend,
Creating magic that knows no end.

Beneath the skies where dreams take form,
Hopes blossom, like winds that warm.
These lighthearted tales remind us, too,
That every heart can start anew.

So gather 'round, both young and old,
For bright adventures, let courage unfold.
In every fable, a lesson shines,
Beneath the stars where laughter intertwines.

In glittering skies, the stories play,
Reminding us to cherish each day.
For lighthearted fables set us free,
Beneath the vast and open sea.

Joyous Radiance in the Forest of Stars

In a forest thick with fragrant pine,
Where night encroaches, stars align.
Each twinkle brings a song to hear,
Radiance shining, drawing near.

With every heartbeats gentle flow,
Magic stirs in the night's glow.
Creatures gather 'neath ancient trees,
In joyous revels, carried with ease.

From deep within the earthly floor,
Whispers rise to the heavens' door.
Here, every wish finds its flight,
In the forest where dreams unite.

With laughter spilling on soft moss beds,
Where time meanders and lightly treads.
The stars reflect on each smiling face,
Crafting connections in this sacred space.

So let your spirit take its chance,
In the forest where starlight dances.
For joy awaits, an endless stream,
In the heart of this wondrous dream.

Glittering Tapestries Woven with Laughter

In gardens where the shadows play,
Laughter dances in the light of day.
With every thread a tale unfurls,
Of magic spun in vibrant swirls.

The heartstrings hum a merry tune,
Beneath the watchful gaze of moon.
Colors blend in joyful art,
Creating bonds that never part.

Beneath the stars, the stories bloom,
As dreams alight in every room.
Woven strong with love and glee,
A tapestry of you and me.

Each giggle glows like fireflies,
A symphony beneath the skies.
A boundless world where we belong,
In laughter's weave, we find our song.

As whispers of the past take flight,
We gather dreams, embraced by night.
With every thread, our hearts entwined,
A tapestry of joy designed.

Mystical Chimes of Radiant Revelry

In twilight's realm, the chimes resound,
Echoes of joy in whispers found.
A symphony of stars above,
That serenades the heart with love.

When shadows stretch and spirits rise,
The night unfolds with secret sighs.
With laughter woven in the air,
We dance like fireflies, unaware.

Each note a glimpse of dreams we've sought,
A melody with magic caught.
Through laughter's lens, the world anew,
Where every heart knows what is true.

In reverie, we share our tales,
As moonlight glimmers, softly sails.
A harmony of hearts in tune,
Beneath the gaze of the silver moon.

With every chime, a wish released,
Our spirits soar, our joys increased.
In this enchanted night we dwell,
With peals of laughter, all is well.

Fantastic Flare of Colorful Whispers

In the hush of dawn, colors collide,
A canvas where our dreams abide.
Whispers brush across the sky,
In brilliant strokes, they soar and fly.

With every hue, a story spins,
A vibrant tapestry begins.
The playful tones of life and fate,
In harmony, they dance and wait.

In gardens lush with shades untold,
Our spirits rise, our hearts unfold.
With every breath, we paint anew,
A world aglow in every hue.

As laughter rings and colors blend,
We find the joy that knows no end.
A symphony of light and cheer,
In whispers bright, we hold you near.

With every stroke, the moments sing,
A flare of life, a joyful thing.
Through whispers soft, our spirits soar,
In colorful dreams, forevermore.

Vivid Streaks of Joy in Enchanted Spaces

In enchanted spaces, magic swirls,
With vivid streaks, the wonder unfurls.
Each corner holds a dream's embrace,
A realm alive with time and space.

Through fields where dreams and laughter run,
We chase the light, we soak in fun.
The vibrant air is thick with cheer,
As joy ignites throughout the sphere.

In every glance, a spark ignites,
Creating memories, pure delights.
With every giggle, every cheer,
The heart feels light, the path made clear.

With whispers soft as morning mist,
The joy we hold cannot be missed.
In trails of laughter, hope takes flight,
A dance of dreams in purest light.

So gather 'round in this embrace,
In vivid joy, find your place.
Through enchanted spaces, spirits soar,
In laughter's warmth, we seek no more.

Prismatic Parables of the Majestic Realm

In a realm where colors fuse,
Echoes of magic gently muse.
Whispers dance in glimmering light,
Secrets bloom in the velvet night.

Beneath the azure skies we tread,
With dreams unfurling, softly spread.
Every shadow, a tale untold,
In vibrant hues, our hearts behold.

Mountains rise with a regal grace,
Time loses track in this wondrous place.
The rivers hum a timeless tune,
Underneath the watchful moon.

Creatures frolic in splendid glee,
Each moment sparkles, wild and free.
With every breeze, the world inspires,
Igniting hopes like dancing fires.

In this realm of prismatic gleam,
Life flows like an enchanting dream.
Together we weave our stories bright,
In the majestic realm of pure delight.

Whimsical Radiance in Twilight's Embrace

As twilight drapes the world in gold,
Stories of wonder begin to unfold.
Stars whisper secrets, soft and slow,
While shadows play in the evening glow.

Moonbeams twirl on the sleeping trees,
Carrying laughter upon the breeze.
Each leaf, a spark in the dusk's delight,
Kindles the magic of the night.

With every step on the mossy floor,
The earth hums tales of lore galore.
The colors blend in a gentle swirl,
As dreams awaken, we dance and twirl.

In this embrace of dusk's sweet song,
We'll find where the dreams of night belong.
With hearts aglow and spirits bright,
We bask in the warmth of fading light.

Here, where the twilight softly sighs,
Whimsical wonders fill the skies.
In the embrace of a night serene,
We wander through realms yet unseen.

Glittering Giggles Beneath Celestial Canopies

Beneath the canopy of shining stars,
Laughter echoes, near and far.
Each giggle sparkles in the night,
Guiding us through realms of light.

The moon smiles down on adventures grand,
As we journey through this dreamy land.
With every twinkle, the cosmos sings,
And grants us hope, on silver wings.

In hidden glades where fairies play,
The secret wishes float away.
With every chuckle, joy takes flight,
As dreams unfold in the soft moonlight.

We chase the shadows, playful and bright,
Through glittering paths in the heart of night.
With warmth around, and love in the air,
Every moment blooms, beyond compare.

So here we dwell, in cosmic cheer,
With glittering giggles, banishing fear.
Under celestial canopies, we explore,
Finding magic forevermore.

Charmed Whispers in the Land of Illusions

In a land where whispers weave,
Magic beckons, hearts believe.
With every step, the world anew,
Filled with wonders, bright and true.

Mirages dance beneath the sun,
Every charm, a tale begun.
Through twilight paths of softest dreams,
Our laughter flows in glimmering streams.

The air is thick with mysteries grand,
As we reach for wonders, hand in hand.
Colorful visions swirl about,
In this land, there's never doubt.

With a flick of thought, the world transforms,
A kaleidoscope of shifting forms.
In every corner, secrets bloom,
Charmed whispers chase away the gloom.

So follow the light, let your heart race,
In this enchanting, hidden space.
For every illusion holds a spark,
In a world where dreams ignite the dark.

Shimmering Tales of the Fantastical Beast

In forests deep where whispers dwell,
A creature roams, its magic spell.
With scales of gold that catch the light,
A guardian fierce, yet gentle in flight.

By moonlit streams, its shadow glides,
With wings unfurled, it softly hides.
A heart of courage wrapped in grace,
In every leap, a world to trace.

Through misty glades, where dreams ignite,
It sings of ancient, starry night.
Each note a charm, each sound a guide,
To realms unseen where wonders bide.

In tales untold, its name shall weave,
A bond of trust, a heart to cleave.
For every beast, a tale awaits,
In shimmering light, where magic fates.

So heed the call of this delight,
For in its gaze, there lies the light.
Embrace the tales, let spirits soar,
For within these woods, there's evermore.

Ethereal Echoes of the Velvet Night

Beneath the stars, in velvet skies,
The night unveils its softest sighs.
Whispers of tales in shadows cast,
Where dreams and memories hold steadfast.

The moon, a lantern, gently glows,
Awakening secrets that nature knows.
Ethereal echoes dance and twir,
In rhythms sweet, like silken fire.

With every breeze, the silence hums,
Of distant lands and ancient drums.
A tapestry of night unfolds,
In silver threads, the darkness holds.

Stars among stars, they flicker bright,
Guiding us through the depths of night.
In soft embrace, the darkness sways,
With ethereal echoes, whispering plays.

So linger here, where time is still,
Embrace the magic, feel the thrill.
For in this night, with dreams alight,
The world awakens in gentle flight.

Glistening Gleams of Otherworldly Lore

In twilight's glow, the stories gleam,
Of lands afar and endless dream.
With every glimmer, a legend wakes,
In whispered truths, the silence breaks.

A tapestry rich, of shadows spun,
Of valor's call and battles won.
In every flicker, a hero stands,
Defying fate with brave commands.

With glisting hues, the canvas glows,
And otherworldly lore bestows.
A bridge of magic between the realms,
Where fantasy and hope overwhelms.

In each soft glow, a truth behold,
Of whispered tales, enchanted gold.
The glistening gleams that light the dawn,
A world reborn, where dreams are drawn.

So raise your gaze to shimmering skies,
And let the magic never die.
For in these stories, we'll always find,
A thread of wonder, forever entwined.

Dazzling Musings from the Shimmering Vale

In shimmering vale, where colors play,
The heart of magic holds its sway.
With every dawn, a story wakes,
In dazzling hues, the dreamer shakes.

Rustling leaves whisper in delight,
As sunbeams dance, a wondrous sight.
Each blade of grass, each petal bold,
Tells tales of lives that time enfold.

In every moment, the breezes tell,
Of hopes and dreams that ring a bell.
Dazzling musings, both fresh and bright,
Awake the spirit, ignite the light.

So wander free through meadows wide,
With open heart, let wonders glide.
In shimmering vale, where dreams are spun,
Find joy in each new day begun.

For within this land, we find our place,
In dazzling musings, a warm embrace.
Let magic shine in every trail,
And whisper softly from the vale.

Sunlit Riddles of the Sapphire Woods

In the heart where sunlight weaves,
Whispers flutter through the leaves.
A shimmering path lies ahead,
Secrets await where the ancients tread.

Mossy stones that tell their tale,
Echoes linger, soft and pale.
The dance of shadows, sweet allure,
For the brave, the woods assure.

Twilight breathes a magic rare,
Fairy lights twinkle in the air.
Riddles wrapped in twilight's glow,
Answers hidden, hush and slow.

Underneath the sprawling sky,
Glimmers of truth drift and fly.
With every step, more is revealed,
The heart of the forest, gently healed.

So wander forth with hopeful heart,
In sapphire woods, let dreams impart.
For the sunlit riddles, vast and wide,
Hold the magic where secrets abide.

Distant Laughter from Stardust Rivers

Across the vale where dreams take flight,
Rivers shimmer under starlit night.
Laughter echoes, a cosmic sound,
In distant realms where joy is found.

Whispers of fate upon the breeze,
Carried forth with flowing ease.
Each ripple holds a story untold,
Of silver wishes and visions bold.

Beneath a sky, vast and wide,
Galaxies dance, side by side.
In twilight's arms, the magic flows,
A tapestry where wonder grows.

With every splash, a wish takes flight,
Underneath the stars so bright.
In stardust rivers, dreams take shape,
And laughter binds the worlds that drape.

So listen close, you'll hear them speak,
Voices soft, both strong and meek.
Distant laughter calls your name,
A celestial tune, eternal flame.

Magical Gleams of Infinite Possibilities

In a world where wishes blaze,
Gleams of magic set ablaze.
Possibilities stretch far and wide,
With every heartbeat, dreams abide.

Colors swirl in vibrant hues,
Thoughts take flight, each spark anew.
The canvas waits for hands to paint,
A tapestry of joy, no feint.

In the silence, echoes swell,
Whispers of secrets yet to tell.
Every heartbeat, a chance to start,
Creating worlds from open heart.

So gather dreams like fireflies,
Chasing shadows under skies.
With every step, new paths arise,
Boundless wonders, sweet surprise.

For in this realm, the sky's the limit,
Infinite possibilities are in it.
So dare to dream and reach for light,
In magical gleams, we take our flight.

Radiant Revelations of the Ethereal Path

Upon the road where starlight glows,
Radiant revelations softly shows.
An ethereal path beneath the stars,
Guides lost souls to heal their scars.

The night unfolds with gentle grace,
In shadows cast, find your place.
Illuminate the darkest fears,
With whispers woven through the years.

Crystal streams of shimmering light,
Lead the way through velvet night.
Each step a dance, each breath a gift,
A chance to feel the spirit lift.

With every turn, new wonders rise,
A symphony beneath the skies.
Follow the glow, don't drift away,
For the ethereal path is here to stay.

So journey forth, embrace the night,
Join the dance, let spirits ignite.
In radiant revelations, find your way,
The heart's true magic, come what may.

Gleams of Laughter in a Magical Tapestry

In a world adorned with colors bright,
Children laugh, their eyes alight.
With every stitch in the fabric spun,
Dreams take flight, like birds that run.

Amidst the threads both strong and fine,
Whispers dance in a soft, sweet line.
Each giggle weaves a story true,
Of friendships deep, of skies so blue.

In forests deep where wonders roam,
Laughter echoes, a magic home.
With pixies playing, shadows cast,
In every heart, the joy will last.

A tapestry rich, where tales entwine,
With each gleam of laughter, we align.
The golden moments softly blend,
Creating magic that will not end.

So gather close, let spirits soar,
In laughter's glow, we find much more.
With every heartbeat, let's embrace,
The woven joy that time won't erase.

Whimsy's Dance on Celestial Waves

Beneath the stars, where secrets play,
Whimsy dances, night and day.
On celestial waves, so bright and free,
Magic twirls, a joyous spree.

With moonlight's touch, and starlit sighs,
Imagination soars, it never lies.
Each ripple sings a song divine,
Of worlds beyond, where wishes shine.

The cosmos hums a gentle tune,
As dreams drift softly, under the moon.
In every heart, the rhythm sways,
A dance of wonder through endless days.

From clouds adorned with silver lace,
To sunsets painting a warm embrace.
Whimsy whispers, a call to roam,
On cosmic tides that lead us home.

So let the winds of fancy guide,
Embrace the magic that won't subside.
Together we'll chase the dreams we crave,
On whimsy's dance, through time's own wave.

Glowing Stories from the Heart of Enchantment

In shadows deep, where secrets dwell,
Glowing stories cast a spell.
With every word, a spark ignites,
Illuminating the darkest nights.

From ancient trees with gnarled roots,
To whispered tales in sylvan shoots,
Each line unfolds a world untold,
Of knights and quests, of treasures bold.

In every corner, magic gleams,
While starlit skies inspire our dreams.
A tapestry of tales to share,
Creating wonders with loving care.

Through valleys lush, where fairies fly,
And echoes of laughter fill the sky,
These glowing stories, rich and wide,
Guide us gently, like the tide.

So listen close, as shadows part,
To the magic thrum within the heart.
In enchanted whispers, we find our way,
To glowing stories that light the day.

Shimmering Sprockets of the Cosmic Play

In the depths where starlight weaves,
Gears of fate begin to spin,
Each moment a glimmered reprieve,
Ticking soft, the dreams within.

Luminous paths twist and twine,
Echoes of laughter fill the air,
Time's embrace draws us in line,
Every wish a whispered prayer.

Charms and spells of cosmic light,
Gliding through the velvet night,
Sprockets spin with ancient might,
Winking stars in playful flight.

Wonders bloom on twilight's seam,
Chasing shadows, dreams awake,
Through the realms of silver dream,
Joyful hearts, no fear, no ache.

So let the cosmic dance begin,
With shimmering sprockets, clear and bright,
In this magical chaos, we spin,
Together in the soft starlight.

Whirls of Whimsy in Glistening Ether

In the mist of woven delight,
Laughter rings through glimmering skies,
Dancing stars, a joyful sight,
As dreams take flight with gentle sighs.

Whirls of whimsy, soft and bright,
Enchantments weave in silver stream,
Chasing light through endless night,
Holding tight to fleeting dreams.

Moonlit echoes twirl and sway,
Sprinkled stardust on our souls,
In this realm where wishes play,
Glistening ether makes us whole.

Through the waves of laughter's song,
Where imaginations brightly bloom,
We dance together, proud and strong,
Hand in hand, we chase the moon.

Let the world spin wild and free,
In this realm of magic's mirth,
For in whimsy, we shall see,
The endless wonders of our worth.

Opalescent Riddles from Mythical Shores

At dawn where legends softly rise,
Opalescent whispers greet the day,
Secrets hide in ocean's sighs,
Mythical shores where shadows play.

Tales of old in currents weave,
Mermaids sing their haunting tune,
In their depths, we dare believe,
Dreams awaken with the moon.

Riddles dance on the salt-kissed air,
Waves caress the timeworn stone,
Wisdom echoes everywhere,
Calling forth the hearts unknown.

Through the mist, a ship appears,
Sails aglow with mystery's thread,
Guided by the hopes and fears,
A journey waits for those who tread.

From mythical shores, we set our quest,
With opalescent dreams held tight,
In the stories, we find rest,
As we sail into the light.

Dance of Light in the Land of Dreams

In the land where starlight twirls,
A dance of light begins to play,
Colors swirl in radiant curls,
Casting shadows, bright and gay.

Endless fields of vibrant hue,
Each step a note in joyful song,
Light and laughter gleam anew,
A wondrous place where we belong.

In the twilight, whispers hum,
As magic flows from heart to heart,
Every moment's beat a drum,
In the dance where dreams impart.

With every sway, the stars align,
Creating paths of pure delight,
In this realm, all souls entwine,
As we twirl beneath the night.

So let us dance, my dear friend,
In the land where dreams take flight,
For in this haven, we transcend,
Forever lost in purest light.

Whispers of Joy in an Arcane Adventure

In a grove where secrets lie,
Faint echoes of laughter sigh.
Mysterious lights flicker and play,
Guiding the brave on their way.

With each wand's flick, a tale unwinds,
Magic dances, and fate unwinds.
Through the mist, a laughter sweet,
Joy blooms where the dreamers meet.

Stars above twinkle with delight,
A promise whispered in the night.
Curious spirits flit and soar,
This adventure opens the door.

Gather the friends, embrace the fire,
Hearts united, rise ever higher.
In this realm where wonder thrives,
Whispers of joy keep hope alive.

So let the unknown be your guide,
In every breath, let magic reside.
With open hearts, the world to explore,
A tapestry woven by dreams of yore.

Banter of Light Among Radiant Shadows

In the twilight, whispers gleam,
Shadows gather, yet hopes beam.
Laughter sparkles like starlit dew,
Banter flows 'tween two and few.

A flicker of fate embraces the night,
As fireflies dance in joyous flight.
Amidst the dark, vibrant sparks play,
Radiant hearts keep the gloom at bay.

With words like spells, we weave our tale,
Through flickering paths where dreams prevail.
Every jest a charm to share,
United by love, beyond compare.

Moments caught in a playful chase,
Light and shadow intertwine in grace.
Through this banter, hope shall grow,
In radiant shadows, let laughter flow.

Lift your spirits, let joy take wing,
In the embrace of night, we sing.
Each heartbeat echoes, a timeless song,
Together in magic, we all belong.

Charming Reflections Beneath a Starry Veil

Beneath the stars, a canvas bright,
Charming whispers fill the night.
Reflections shimmer on the lake,
Dreams unfold with every wake.

Glistening pixies dance in glee,
Painting hopes for all to see.
With each splash, a story flows,
In golden light, the magic grows.

Time seems lost, yet never ends,
In midnight's arms, the spirit mends.
With laughter sweet and joy entwined,
Under a veil, our hearts aligned.

Gathered here in starlit grace,
We find our dreams in this sacred place.
With every glance, a tale is spun,
Charming reflections, we've just begun.

So let the night weave its charm anew,
As we cherish the beauty in all we do.
With each heartbeat, let sorcery blend,
For beneath the stars, love has no end.

Dazzling Jests in the Realm of Wonder

In a realm where the fantastical sings,
Dazzling jests take flight on bright wings.
Laughter echoes through crystal halls,
As feast and folly enchant us all.

Magical creatures romp and play,
In shimmering light, they find their way.
Through forests deep and castles grand,
Wonder blooms at their command.

Every joke a spell well cast,
With joy's embrace, our fears are past.
In vibrant hues, our spirits soar,
In this realm we shall explore.

Gather the mirth, let the merry ring,
Unlock the enchantment that joy can bring.
For in our hearts, the magic spreads,
With dazzling jests, no shadow treads.

So dance and revel, let laughter flow,
In the realm of wonder, let kindness grow.
Each moment cherished, never small,
Together in fun, we shall have it all.

Iridescent Murmurs of the Magical Forest

In a grove where whispers blend,
The trees bend low with stories to send.
Glowing lights dance on evening's breath,
Casting shadows of dreams entwined with depth.

Soft echoes of laughter drift on the breeze,
Among enchanted blooms and ancient trees.
Each shimmer a promise, a tale to be spun,
In this forest of magic where all is begun.

Toadstools adorn the mossy floor,
Each step reveals a mythical lore.
Creatures peek from behind every stone,
In their secret world, never alone.

Stars above twinkle, a celestial guide,
Leading lost souls through the night, untried.
With a flick of a wand and a chant so bold,
The forest unveils its wonders untold.

In this realm where the unbelievable gleams,
The heart dances wild, and the spirit dreams.
Breathe deeply the magic, let your heart soar,
For in this forest, you'll discover much more.

Beacons of Joy in Fable's Light

In stories woven of heart and delight,
Lies a tapestry bright in fable's light.
With each page turned, new wonders awake,
A world where the wishes of dreamers can take.

Winding paths of cobblestone glow,
With laughter and whispers that only kids know.
Glistening eyes of the creatures we meet,
Show the magic that bubbles in every heartbeat.

Candles of hope in lanterns hung high,
Guide every wanderer beneath the vast sky.
With tales that soar, and verses that sing,
These beacons of joy bring summer and spring.

From castles grand to valleys below,
Every tale penned makes imaginations grow.
In corners of pages, dreams take their flight,
Leaving traces of love in the soft, starry night.

So gather your dreams, let your spirit take wing,
For life is the fable, and joy is the zing.
In the glow of the stories we cherish and write,
We find ourselves dancing in fable's warm light.

Twinkling Chronicles of the Whimsical Realm

In a fetch of stars on a velvet night,
Chronicles shimmer, all aglow with light.
Pixies flitter, their laughter rings clear,
In this whimsical realm where all hearts draw near.

Each tale unfolds like petals in spring,
With secrets wrapped tight in the songs that they sing.
Mountains of candy and rivers of ink,
In this place of wonders, we pause and think.

Magic spills forth from every corner,
On the back of a dragon, or sweet-coated mourner.
Embrace the enchantment that often feels near,
For the whimsical realm thrives on love, not fear.

Every creature a muse, every whisper a dream,
Launching our hearts on a sparkling stream.
Time's gentle hands can soften the sound,
As stories awaken, forever unbound.

So journey with joy through this mystical land,
Let the chronicles twinkle, and dreams expand.
For with every laugh and each joyful scream,
We weave our own magic, igniting the dream.

Enchanted Chuckles in Moonlit Meadows

Moonlight dances on the meadow's embrace,
Where laughter and echoes weave a soft grace.
A chorus of crickets begins their sweet song,
In enchanted fields where shadows belong.

Stars sprinkle silver on petals so bright,
Each blossom a beacon in the cool, gentle night.
The softest of sighs drift across the land,
Carrying whispers where wishes are planned.

Breezes tickle the boughs, giggles in the air,
While fireflies twinkle without any care.
In the heart of the darkness, joy finds its reign,
In these moonlit meadows, laughter will gain.

Gather the giggles, let spirits ignite,
As dreams intertwine in the shimmering light.
Every chuckle a spell, every grin a delight,
In these enchanted moments, hearts take flight.

So dance through the meadows and revel in cheer,
For the beauty of laughter is destined to steer.
In the glow of the moon, we craft our own fate,
With enchanted chuckles, let love captivate.

Flickering Smiles on a Unicorn's Trail

In a realm where dreams take flight,
Unicorns dance beneath the moonlight.
Flickering smiles they leave behind,
Whispers of magic to help you find.

Tails of silver, manes of gold,
Stories of wonders yet untold.
Each step they take, a spark in the night,
Guiding the lost to the source of light.

Through fields of daisies, soft and bright,
Laughter echoes, hearts take flight.
Flickering smiles, a shared delight,
Spreading warmth like the morning light.

With every gallop, a promise made,
Of joy and love that will not fade.
In this realm, where magic blends,
Flickering smiles, where the heart mends.

So follow the trail, let your heart be bold,
Find the treasures that cannot be sold.
For in each smile, a story waits,
On a unicorn's trail, joy creates.

Adventures in the Glow of Starlight

Under skies adorned with golden stars,
Adventures beckon, both near and far.
In the glow of night, dreams seem real,
Whispers of magic that time can heal.

With friends beside us, laughter shared,
We wander boldly, unprepared.
Each step a chance, each turn a thrill,
Chasing stardust on the night's soft chill.

Moonlit pathways beneath our feet,
Guiding our journey, a melody sweet.
Through stories woven in twilight's embrace,
We find ourselves in this starlit space.

From the tallest peaks to valleys wide,
In every heartbeat, the universe hides.
Mysteries wrapped in night's gentle shroud,
Bringing forth courage, making us proud.

So dance beneath the twinkling skies,
With every adventure, a chance to rise.
In the glow of starlight, we forge our fate,
Together we'll wander, it's never too late.

Lively Banter Across Celestial Fields

In the whispering winds of the night,
Lively banter takes to flight.
Across celestial fields we roam,
Where stars gather, and call us home.

With laughter ringing beneath the stars,
We share our dreams, unbroken bars.
Thoughts like comets streak through the sky,
Illuminating hopes that soar high.

Hand in hand, we chase the dawn,
Where every moment feels like a yawn.
In this symphony of whimsy and cheer,
We find the courage to push through fear.

Through valleys of light, our spirits race,
Every corner turned, a warm embrace.
In friendship found, the heart beats strong,
Together we weave the universe's song.

So let the banter continue to flow,
In celestial fields where wildflowers grow.
With every laugh, a new tale we spin,
In the magic of night, where journeys begin.

Enchanted Illuminations of Joyous Tales

In the heart of night, where dreams take hold,
Enchanted illuminations shine like gold.
Joyous tales dance in the moon's soft glow,
Waiting to whisper the stories we know.

With every flicker of the candle's flame,
Legends awaken, calling our name.
From ancient woods to the shimmering sea,
The magic unfolds, wild and free.

In laughter's embrace, we lose our way,
In each story told, we find our sway.
Fables of love, of courage, of dreams,
Flow through the night like enchanting streams.

So gather 'round, let the tales be spun,
Under the backdrop of the night's soft run.
In every heartbeat, light shall prevail,
With enchanted illuminations of joyous tales.

As starlight blankets the world in peace,
May the stories linger, never cease.
For in every tale, we carve our mark,
In the tapestry of night, our spirits spark.

Smiles in the Silhouettes of Myth

In shadows deep where stories blend,
Mythical whispers around me send.
Creatures dance on moonlit ground,
In every tale, enchantments found.

A dragon's roar, a siren's song,
In twilight's grasp, we all belong.
For every heart that dares to dream,
Finds solace in the twilight seam.

With every step, the whispers grow,
On paths of light where magic flows.
From ancient woods to heights of grace,
In every myth, we find our place.

The fae weave spells with gossamer thread,
In every story, the past is wed.
So close your eyes, let wonders guide,
For in this world, fears subside.

With smiles bright in silhouettes,
Of mythic lore, our spirits met.
Together we'll create our fate,
In dreams that soar, we celebrate.

Delightful Glisten of Reveries Unspooled

Delightful glimmers kiss the night,
As reveries take their gentle flight.
Threads of silver in whispers weave,
Tales of wonder, hearts believe.

The starlit paths of dreams unfold,
In every moment, a story told.
Glimpses of joy, like morning dew,
Each drop reflecting shades anew.

As laughter dances on the breeze,
It carries hopes with graceful ease.
Lost in visions, we drift and sway,
In tranquil pools where thoughts can play.

With every glance, the world ignites,
In vibrant hues, our spirit fights.
Through fields of dreams, we wander free,
In every heartbeat, it's you and me.

So cherish each delightful gleam,
In waking moments, let us dream.
For life's a tapestry with threads,
Of dreams that glisten, never shed.

Glittery Memories from the Realm of Dreams

In twilight's clasp, where memories gleam,
We journey far, dance in a dream.
With each soft sigh, the past emerges,
In swirling mists where magic surges.

Glittery echoes of laughter ring,
As time does twist, it takes to wing.
In shadows bright, we find our threads,
A tapestry of all that spreads.

From hidden glades to castles high,
We chase the stars across the sky.
In every glance, a secret shared,
In dreams, we find what once was bared.

With twinkling light, our spirits soar,
In glittery memories, we explore.
A treasure trove of what has been,
In every heart, a spark within.

So hold the moments, cherish the glow,
From realms afar, where wonders flow.
In every heartbeat, and every sigh,
Glittery dreams will never die.

Enchanted Whimsy Beneath a Cosmic Blanket

Beneath the sky where stardust glows,
An enchanted whimsy gently flows.
With every twinkle, a new delight,
In cosmic dreams, we take our flight.

The night unfolds like velvet sails,
As whispered wishes travel trails.
With laughter bright like fireflies,
We wander where the magic lies.

Each shooting star, a hopeful sign,
In cosmic dance, our spirits twine.
With every heartbeat, secrets shared,
In hidden realms, love is declared.

So let us lay 'neath this grand embrace,
With starlit dreams, we find our place.
In every spark, a story spins,
In whimsies woven, our journey begins.

With every sigh, the cosmos sings,
In enchanted tales, the heart takes wings.
A universe where laughter stays,
Beneath the blanket of endless days.

www.ingramcontent.com/pod-product-compliance
Ingram Content Group UK Ltd.
Pitfield, Milton Keynes, MK11 3LW, UK
UKHW021326280125
4330UKWH00005B/421